TWO TRUTHS AND A MYTH

THE Boston TEA PARTY

SPOT THE MYTHS

by Megan Cooley Peterson

CAPSTONE PRESS
a capstone imprint

Published by Capstone Press, an imprint of Capstone
1710 Roe Crest Drive
North Mankato, Minnesota 56003
capstonepub.com

Copyright © 2025 by Capstone. All rights reserved. No part of this publication may be reproduced in whole or in part, or stored in a retrieval system, or transmitted in any form or by any means, electronic, mechanical, photocopying, recording, or otherwise, without written permission of the publisher.

Library of Congress Cataloging-in-Publication Data
is available on the Library of Congress website.
ISBN: 9781669087090 (hardcover)
ISBN: 9781669087045 (paperback)
ISBN: 9781669087052 (ebook PDF)

Summary: After the Boston Tea Party in 1773, myths about the event emerged. Did a raise in tea taxes lead up to the event? Did the colonists dump full tea crates into the sea? Now it's up to you to separate the truths from the myths. Will you be able to guess them, or will you be fooled?

Editorial Credits
Editor: Carrie Sheely; Designer: Elyse White; Media Researcher: Jo Miller; Production Specialist: Tori Abraham

Image Credits
Alamy: Ivy Close Images, 9, The Reading Rome, 11, World History Archive, 12; Bridgeman Images/Philadelphia History Museum at the Atwater Kent/Courtesy of Historical Society of Pennsylvania Collection, 29; Getty Images: duncan1890, 15, 17, 25, Edward Gooch Collection, 24, Hulton Archive, 13, 21, 7, Popperfoto, 23, MPI, 28; Library of Congress, cover, 4, 19; SuperStock: Everett Collection, 27

Design Elements: Getty Images: TheresaTibbetts; Shutterstock: cTermit, Malenkka, Valentina Vectors, Valeriia Soloveva

Source Notes
Page 11, "This meeting can do . . .," Gabrielle Emanuel, "The Boston Tea Party at 250: History Steeped in Myth," WBUR, December 14, 2023, https://www.wbur.org/news/2023/12/14/boston-tea-party-anniversary-fact-fiction, Accessed June 11, 2024.

Any additional websites and resources referenced in this book are not maintained, authorized, or sponsored by Capstone. All product and company names are trademarks™ or registered® trademarks of their respective holders.

TABLE OF CONTENTS

What Really Happened at the Boston Tea Party? 4

Before the Tea Party 6

Boston's Main Players 10

The East India Company 14

Heading to the Ships 18

Spilling the Tea 22

After the Tea Party 26

Glossary 30
Read More 31
Internet Sites 31
Index 32
About the Author 32

Words in **bold** are in the glossary.

What Really Happened at the Boston Tea Party?

It's December 16, 1773, at Griffin's Wharf in the Massachusetts Bay **Colony**. In the cover of darkness, several dozen men sneak onto three ships docked there. The ships are carrying tea from Great Britain. The men dump as much tea as they can overboard.

These American colonists were **protesting** the British government. The British government had passed laws about the handling of tea being **imported** to the colonies. The colonists had no say in British government. They believed the laws were unfair.

The men soon destroyed 342 crates of tea. This act brought the colonists one step closer to war with Britain.

Onlookers watch protesters dump tea during the Boston Tea Party.

After the event, myths were born. How much do you know about the Boston Tea Party? Three statements will be presented together. But only two are true. Do your best to decide what's truth and what's a myth. How well will you play the game?

HOW CAN I TELL WHAT'S TRUTH AND WHAT'S A MYTH?

START HERE. ⇨ Does the statement include words like "all" or "none"?

YES ⇨ It might be a myth. Words such as "all" or "none" often simplify complicated topics. These statements might not be true.

NO ⇨ Does the statement include specific information, such as names or dates?

YES ⇨ It might be true. Details are important when dealing with facts. The more details a statement provides, the more likely it is to be true.

NO ⇨ It might be a myth. Vague facts without detail might be made up. It's good to question statements that don't include specific details.

Before the Tea Party

TRUTH OR MYTH?

1. MANY COLONIAL TEA MERCHANTS SOLD SMUGGLED TEA INSTEAD OF BRITISH TEA.

Only British tea was taxed. Dutch tea **smuggled** into the colonies avoided the tea tax. Smugglers hid the illegal tea from port officials. If caught, smugglers could lose their ship and cargo.

2. COLONISTS TARRED AND FEATHERED THOSE WHO SUPPORTED THE TEA TAX.

To show their disapproval, colonists covered the tax supporters with hot, sticky tar. Then they dumped feathers on them. The practice was painful and embarrassing for victims.

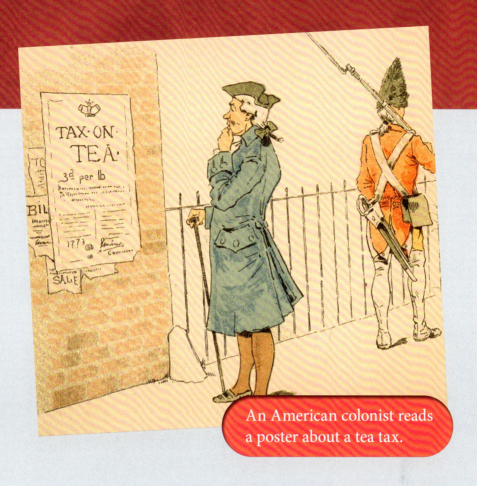

An American colonist reads a poster about a tea tax.

3. THE BRITISH GOVERNMENT VOTED TO INCREASE THE TEA TAX IN MAY 1773.

After the tax increase, legally imported tea became too costly for most colonists. They had to buy smuggled tea.

THE MYTH

THE BRITISH GOVERNMENT VOTED TO INCREASE THE TEA TAX IN MAY 1773.

The British government passed the Tea Act in May 1773. This new law did not raise the tea tax. In fact, it made British tea cheaper. The Tea Act gave the British East India Company a **monopoly** on tea sales in the colonies. They could sell their tea directly to American shop owners. This cut out American tea merchants. They were upset Great Britain was interfering with their business.

The Townshend Acts of 1767 first introduced the tea tax. These laws taxed goods from England, such as glass, paper, paint, and tea. Colonists felt these taxes were unfair. They wanted a say in how and when the British government could tax them.

Colonists refused to buy many British goods, including tea. Their **boycott** worked. Most of the Townshend Acts were cancelled in 1770. The tea tax, however, was not. The tea boycott continued, even after the Tea Act lowered tea prices. The colonists did not want to be controlled by the British government.

FACT

In 1770, Boston children bothered British soldiers who were there in support of tax laws. The children even threw oyster shells and snowballs at the soldiers.

Boston's Main Players

TRUTH OR MYTH?

1. BY 1765, COLONISTS HAD FORMED A SECRET GROUP CALLED THE SONS OF LIBERTY TO UNDERMINE BRITISH RULE.

The Sons of Liberty opposed British taxes. One of the first taxes it opposed was the Stamp Act of 1765. The act meant colonists had to pay a tax on paper documents such as newspapers. The group quickly gained members from around the colonies. In late 1773, armed members would not allow ships to unload their British tea. The tea tax went unpaid.

2. GOVERNOR THOMAS HUTCHINSON BANNED TEA SHIPS FROM LEAVING BOSTON WITHOUT UNLOADING AND PAYING THE TAX.

The British government could take the ships and the tea if the owners refused to unload. But angry colonists did not want the ships unloaded. Ship owners were stuck in the middle.

3. SONS OF LIBERTY LEADER SAMUEL ADAMS GAVE THE SIGNAL TO TOSS THE TEA.

Thousands of people met at the Old South Meeting House the night of the Tea Party. "This meeting can do nothing more to save the country," Adams told the audience. When he said "country," Adams meant the colonies. This was the call to dump the tea.

The Old South Meeting House was one of the largest buildings in Boston in the 1770s.

FACT

Loaded tea ships trying to return to England risked being gunned down by British troops.

THE MYTH

THE MYTH: SONS OF LIBERTY LEADER SAMUEL ADAMS GAVE THE SIGNAL TO TOSS THE TEA.

On November 27, the first Tea Party ship carrying East India tea arrived at Boston Harbor. At a meeting the next day, Dr. Thomas Young proposed dumping the tea overboard. Samuel Adams rejected that idea. He wanted to send the ship back to England without unloading the tea. All the meeting members passed Adams's proposal.

Leaders at the meeting the night of the Tea Party had to keep order over the huge crowd.

Samuel Adams

Why did the colonists dump the tea anyway? Perhaps this group rejected Adams's call to send the tea back. Some say war whoops immediately sounded outside after Adams spoke his famous line. Yet others say the whoops didn't happen until several minutes later. Adams was reported to have warned everyone to ignore the shouts and stay inside.

It is quite possible Samuel Adams wanted the rebels to toss the tea. But there's no historical proof he gave a direct order.

The East India Company

TRUTH OR MYTH?

1. THE EAST INDIA COMPANY WAS CLOSE TO GOING BANKRUPT.

The colonists' tea boycott hurt the East India Company. East India warehouses held 17 million pounds (7.7 million kilograms) of unsold tea.

2. GOVERNOR THOMAS HUTCHINSON HANDPICKED EAST INDIA TEA AGENTS IN BOSTON.

Hutchinson was loyal to the British government. He chose his sons, friends, and relatives to sell the tea to shop owners. This made many colonists angry.

3. THE BRITISH GOVERNMENT OWNED THE EAST INDIA TEA ON BOARD THE SHIPS IN GRIFFIN'S WHARF ON DECEMBER 16, 1773.

Great Britain also owned the ships. Dumping the tea was a direct attack against the British government.

In 1765, Thomas Hutchinson fled when people angry about the Stamp Act broke into his house.

15

THE MYTH

THE BRITISH GOVERNMENT OWNED THE EAST INDIA TEA ON BOARD THE SHIPS IN GRIFFIN'S WHARF ON DECEMBER 16, 1773.

The tea the colonists dumped did not belong to Great Britain. The East India Company owned the tea. It was Britain's second-largest company. The British government did not own any of the ships that were raided either. The *Dartmouth*, *Eleanor*, and *Beaver* were privately owned by American colonists.

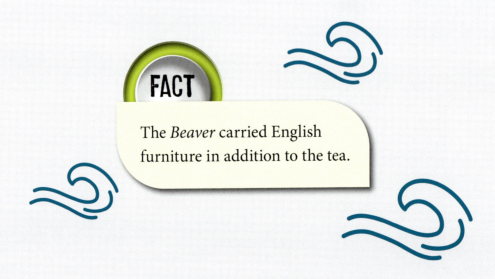

FACT

The *Beaver* carried English furniture in addition to the tea.

The *Dartmouth* (center) was carrying 114 chests of tea at the time of the Boston Tea Party.

Francis Rotch co-owned the *Dartmouth* and *Beaver* with his father, Joseph. They earned a living shipping whale oil to Great Britain. They were paid to bring East India tea back to the colonies. The *Dartmouth* was the first Tea Party ship to arrive in Boston. Samuel Adams and other Boston leaders demanded Rotch return the tea to England. They said if he unloaded the tea, bad things might happen. Rotch asked Governor Thomas Hutchinson for safe passage back to England. The governor said no. Rotch and the other owners decided to keep their ships fully loaded.

Heading to the Ships

TRUTH OR MYTH?

1. ALL RAIDING COLONISTS DRESSED UP AS MEMBERS OF THE MOHAWK PEOPLE.

The colonists wore this clothing as they marched to the ships. By looking like **Indigenous** people, the colonists were harder to recognize. They didn't want to be punished.

2. RAIDING COLONISTS SAFELY LED THE SHIP CREWS OFF BOARD.

The colonists didn't want the ships' crew members to be hurt. Colonists also made sure customs agents were brought somewhere safe. These workers collected taxes at port.

3. MORE THAN 1,000 PEOPLE WATCHED THE TEA PARTY UNFOLD.

The crowd stood a safe distance from the ships. They were quiet as they watched, much like the raiders on board.

The large crowd watching the Boston Tea Party spilled out onto docks.

THE MYTH

ALL RAIDING COLONISTS DRESSED UP AS MEMBERS OF THE MOHAWK PEOPLE.

Many colonists wore Indigenous clothing the night of the Tea Party. But the clothing probably wasn't specific to any group. The Mohawk people lived in the New York area. People in Boston were probably unfamiliar with them. They wouldn't have known what their clothing looked like.

The raiders likely wore disguises of all kinds. One Boston merchant said many raiders wore blankets over their heads. They smeared dark soot on their faces. They all agreed to keep their identities a secret.

FACT

The identities of many Tea Party participants remain a mystery to this day.

Boston Tea Party protesters disguised as Indigenous people prepare to dump tea.

Spilling the Tea

TRUTH OR MYTH?

1. THE COLONISTS TOSSED FULL CRATES OF TEA INTO BOSTON HARBOR.

The crates were small and easy for the raiders to toss overboard. They floated on the water's surface before sinking.

2. TRAINED MILITIA PROTECTED THE RAIDERS.

Boston merchant John Hancock led a group called the Corps of Cadets. These armed cadets kept the rebels safe. Some even helped toss the tea.

3. ON A SHIP, A MAN TRIED TO POCKET SOME TEA.

The man, Charles Conner, was caught. Men removed his coat, smeared him with mud, and beat him.

Protesters may have rowed in small boats to get from shore to the ships carrying tea.

THE MYTH

THE COLONISTS TOSSED FULL CRATES OF TEA INTO BOSTON HARBOR.

The raiding colonists wanted to dump as much tea as possible. But they had to work quickly. They were committing a crime. They didn't want to get caught or go to jail.

Each crate of tea weighed more than 400 pounds (180 kg). Lugging them by hand onto the deck would have taken too long. The men used the ships' tackles and ropes to lift each crate from the **hold**. The men broke open the crates with axes. Others hauled the crates to the ships' railings. They spilled the loose tea overboard.

Boston Tea Party protesters break open the tea crates with axes.

Tea pours out of the crates into the water during the Boston Tea Party.

Many popular illustrations show colonists tossing tea into the water. But the **tide** was low that night. The tea landed in the mud. It began to pile up. Some raiders went over the sides of the ships to flatten the tea. Once the tide rose, tea leaves floated in the water.

The raiders swept the ships' decks after dumping the tea. They even replaced a padlock that had been damaged.

After the Tea Party

TRUTH OR MYTH?

1. AMERICAN COLONISTS CELEBRATED THE BOSTON TEA PARTY.

Colonial leaders praised the Tea Party rebels. Their act of rebellion against Great Britain led directly to the American Revolution.

2. THE BRITISH GOVERNMENT CLOSED BOSTON HARBOR IN JUNE 1774.

British officials wanted to punish the colonists. They also sent British troops to the city. The harbor remained closed until 1776 when British troops left Boston.

3. Colonists dumped more tea into the Boston Harbor in March 1774.

Colonists also dumped tea in other cities, such as New York and Charleston, South Carolina. What happened in Boston inspired people in other cities to protest.

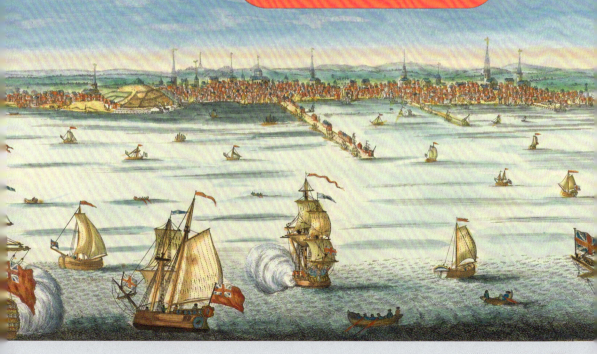

Many ships brought goods to the port of Boston in the late 1700s.

THE MYTH

AMERICAN COLONISTS CELEBRATED THE BOSTON TEA PARTY.

The destroyed tea would have been worth about $1 million today. Many colonists, including George Washington, viewed the raiders as thieves. The event wasn't even called the "Boston Tea Party" until decades later.

After the Tea Party, the British government passed the Intolerable Acts. These acts included closing Boston Harbor and forcing Boston to pay for the ruined tea. These acts also gave land north of the Ohio River to Canada. Some wealthy colonists owned land there. They lost their land and money. Many colonists became even more angry with Great Britain's actions.

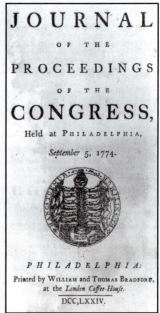

A journal cover from the First Continental Congress

Colonial leaders formed the First Continental Congress in September 1774. They came up with a plan to protest the Intolerable Acts. In April 1775, the American Revolution began.

Participants in the First Continental Congress met at Carpenters' Hall in Philadelphia.

More than 250 years ago, Boston colonists destroyed tea shipped from England. This act pushed the colonies one step closer to independence. Many myths were born that cold night in December 1773. How many did you spot?

FACT

When the Boston Port closed, other colonies shipped needed supplies to Boston.

GLOSSARY

boycott (BOY-kot)—to refuse to buy or use a product or service to protest something believed to be wrong or unfair

colony (KAH-luh-nee)—a territory settled by people from another country and controlled by that country

hold (HOHLD)—the cargo space inside of a ship

import (IM-port)—to bring goods into one country from another

Indigenous (in-DI-juh-nuhs)—a way to describe the first people who lived in a certain area

monopoly (muh-NAH-puh-lee)—a situation in which there is only one supplier of a good or service so that supplier can control the price

protest (pro-TEST)—to object to something strongly and publicly

smuggle (SMUHG-uhl)—to bring something into or out of a country illegally

tide (TYDE)—the rising and falling of the ocean up and down the shore; there are usually two high tides and two low tides in one day

READ MORE

Anderson, Ted. *The Boston Tea Party*. North Mankato, MN: Capstone, 2021.

Hansen, Grace. *Living Through the Revolutionary War*. Minneapolis: DiscoverRoo, an imprint of Pop!, 2024.

Marciniak, Kristin. *12 Incredible Facts About the Boston Tea Party*. Mankato, MN: Black Rabbit Books, 2025.

INTERNET SITES

Boston Tea Party Ships & Museum
bostonteapartyship.com

History.com: Boston Tea Party
history.com/topics/american-revolution/boston-tea-party

*National Constitution Center: On This Day,
the Boston Tea Party Lights a Fuse*
constitutioncenter.org/blog/on-this-day-the-boston-tea-party
-lights-a-fuse

INDEX

Adams, Samuel, 11, 12, 13, 17
American Revolution, 26, 29

Boston Harbor, 12, 22, 24, 26, 27, 28
boycotts, 9, 14

East India Company, 8, 12, 14, 15, 16, 17

First Continental Congress, 28, 29

Griffin's Wharf, 4, 15, 16

Hutchinson, Thomas, 10, 14, 15, 17

Indigenous people, 18, 20, 21
Intolerable Acts, 28, 29

Old South Meeting House, 11

Rotch, Francis, 17

smuggled tea, 6, 7
Sons of Liberty, 10, 11, 12
Stamp Act, 10, 15

Tea Act, 8, 9
Townshend Acts, 8, 9

Washington, George, 28

ABOUT THE AUTHOR

Megan Cooley Peterson is a writer, editor, and bookworm. When she isn't writing or reading, you can find her watching movies or planning her next Halloween party. She lives in Minnesota with her husband and daughter.